TOM CHIVE~

Tom Chiv...   ...in south London in 1983. He is the author of *How to Build a*
City (Salt ...   ...09), *The Terrors* (Nine Arches, 2009; shortlisted for the Michael
Marks Aw...   ... Pamphlets), *Flood Drain* (Annexe Press, 2014) and, as editor,
the antho...   ...*te: New London Poetry* and *Adventures in Form* (Penned in the
Margins, ...   He won an Eric Gregory Award in 2011, and was shortlisted
for the F...   ...Award in 2014. As well as founding Penned in the Margins, he
co-dire...   ...rd Festival from 2008 to 2011.

Marginalia

Ten Years of Poems & Texts from Penned in the Margins

Penned in the Margins

LONDON

PUBLISHED BY PENNED IN THE MARGINS
Toynbee Studios, 28 Commercial Street, London E1 6AB
www.pennedinthemargins.co.uk

First published 2014

Printed in the United Kingdom by Bell & Bain Ltd.

ISBN
978-1-908058-20-1

CONTENTS

FOREWORD

ON 20ᵗʜ AUGUST 2004, in a dank basement underneath the railway in Herne Hill, South London, I introduced a group of ten poets to an audience of friends and locals. Fresh out of university, I figured myself a dabbler in the dark arts of language: producing a small magazine (*Keystone*), helping out with another (*Tears in the Fence*), and of course writing poems of my own. The night was called 'Penned in the Margins': a phrase lifted, self-indulgently, from one of those poems: '*I Guthlac / steadfast on my island / in my insularity / stamping at boundaries / lost contours of march / penned in the margins.*'

Ten years on and, like the Anglo-Saxon hermit-saint, I'm still stamping at boundaries; no longer in a dank basement but working from a small office in East London on publications and performances for people who are not afraid to take risks.

In a phrase repeated so often it almost seems apocryphal, Iain Sinclair described the British poetry scene as 'a knife fight in a phone booth'. Penned in the Margins was conceived as a publisher that looked beyond small-minded factionalism to promote the full diversity of poetries in Britain. We have built a publishing stable that comprises performance poets (Luke Wright, Ross Sutherland), experimental poets (SJ Fowler, Emily Critchley), lyric poets (Sarah Hesketh, Melissa Lee-Houghton, Roddy Lumsden) and some who resist categorisation altogether (Hannah Silva, Siddhartha Bose).

Penned in the Margins has sometimes been called 'alternative'; and that's fine by me. Our relationship to mainstream literary culture has always been provisional, on the edge of things. Writing in *Poetry London*, Philip Gross described *City State: New London Poetry* as 'a central space that is also the meeting place of many edges'; in *Poetry Review* Katy Evans-Bush declared *Adventures in Form* to be 'the start of a new, healthier and more joyous way of looking at the poetic endeavour.' The last couple of years has brought wider recognition in the form of Poetry Book Society selections for *Adventures in Form*, *Beautiful Girls* by Melissa Lee-Houghton and Meghan Purvis's translation of *Beowulf*, and the longlisting of Claire Trévien's collection *The Shipwrecked House* for the Guardian First Book Award. With over forty titles now under my belt, Penned in the Margins is based in Toynbee Studios where I am ably supported by Production and Research Assistant Nick Murray. Our publications reach a wide audience thanks to our distributor Central Books and our sales agent Inpress Books, and we have been fortunate in working with talented book designers: Ian Simmonds, Will Daw and, most recently, Ben Anslow.

Authors are the life-blood of any publishing company, and over the past decade I am proud to have built up an eclectic group of writers from all over the country, writing from many different contexts. Many of them I would rank as friends as well as collaborators. Editing is an unfashionable concept in an industry increasingly driven by the demands of marketing, but it is integral to my approach as a publisher. It signals a commitment to the author, and to the reading experience, that I hope shines through the text.

Central to my vision is literature as language-in-performance, existing not as an isolated species but in a fluid dynamic with theatre, music, comedy, live arts, and with new digital media. Penned in the Margins has always created events and productions alongside, and often in collaboration with, our publishing programme. In Marginalia there many poets whose work can be found off as well as on the page: Luke Wright, Siddhartha Bose, SJ Fowler, Hannah Silva and Ross Sutherland. Our very first perfect-bound book, *Generation Txt*, was the basis for a nationwide live poetry tour. Most recently we have collaborated with Claire Trévien to transform *The Shipwrecked House* into a multi-sensory theatre piece complete with ropes, pulleys and two specially commissioned perfumes.

This anthology is a celebration. Less of a 'Best of' and more of a 'Now That's What I Call...' A poetry mix-tape, lovingly recorded, with your name scrawled on the front in biro. My choices were, as ever, subjective and capricious; I did not consult with the authors but just followed my instincts. There is no single theme, though you might identify some recurrent motifs - the body, the city, our shifting relationship with language and modernity. Some texts here have 'done the rounds'. I think of Ross Sutherland's 'Two Moons for Mongs', for instance - possibly the best, and funniest, example of a contemporary univocalism. Others selections will, I hope, surprise both readers and authors.

The poems that follow range in location from Dark Age Denmark to twenty-first century Mumbai; from rural Dorset to contemporary London (filtered, variously, through Google Streetview, a glass of water and a Saturday night on the town). In form they morph and twist, some adopting and adapting traditional forms, others coalescing into prose blocks or fracturing across the page in unconstrained textual sculptures. Some are expansive, discursive or conversational; others (such as Roddy Lumsden's short lyrics) arrive as compressed, honed nuggets of language. And alongside the poetry that makes up the bulk of our back catalogue, you will find excerpts from prose works by Luke Kennard, Alan Cunningham, Gemma Seltzer and Heather Phillipson.

Penned in the Margins stands for the power of words to challenge how we think, test new ideas and explore alternative stories. There is, within these pages, political observation, compelling social satire, history, humour and poem-as-play - but always, I hope, there is language brought to bear on the world and on the self.

Tom Chivers
Editor
London, August 2014

Marginalia

Hwaet
Meghan Purvis

            Stop me
if you've heard this one before: the lands up north,
hoar-bent, frost-locked, need deeper plows
to dig them. Here is one.

Austerity rules, okay!
Steve Spence

I have been here too long but I have yet to find a
suitable guide who can guess where I am going.
Cash remains the most important method of payment
for small transactions yet their manifesto promises
to maintain current levels of defence spending.
Successful applicants will be required to provide
an enhanced disclosure. It is low tide and directly
below the doorway the shore lies exposed. Fifteen
miles off the coast a sea turtle is seen struggling
through the slick. Coral reefs in many parts of the
world now face devastation yet she is as trendily
crisp and flawlessly groomed as you might expect.
To qualify, simply switch to our high interest
account using our hassle-free switching service.

When Paperboys Roamed the Earth
Ross Sutherland

Your scrappy Reeboks are the first to break the frost;
a bicycle track surgically stitching our hollow streets together.
And nobody knows these bungalows better.
Each detail of our back gardens: the debris of playthings;
hoarded bricks that refused to be barbecues;
ripped cans and wet ashtrays.
Picking past croquet hoops and dog shit,
you navigate our traps
to pass daily judgement on our novelty doormats.

From the daily exchange at our letterbox,
it seems you have become a connoisseur of us.
You know when our children have brought home a fuck,
how the widowers smell different from the divorcees,
the death of a goldfish instantly broadcast
by the condensation on our toilet windows.

Your satchel maps our pavement politics,
exposing a secret vein of *Times* readers,
shifting into salmon as the fences rise.
Blotches of red-tops fester in cul-de-sacs;
both a *Guardian* and a *Sun* for the Fitzpatricks at 12,
their conversation like tectonic plates across the breakfast bar.

Next door, J. Bruce stuffs yesterday's *Mail* into sodden brogues, property pages retained for the post-Evensong massacre of spiders.

Smoke rises from the scrub. The telegraph poles
end here— this is as far as word can travel.
Back in bed, you compile your report in dreams.
Dogs bark instructions at the moon.
Polished umber cars are unlocked at a distance.
Men with windy faces watch ducks raping ducks
on recently reshingled driveways
as Tuesday arrives. A thousand bald patches begin to itch.
An egg boils. Here is the news.

The Machine
Roddy Lumsden

An egg when
cooked is all tails. Wink into its one yellow eye and see

its spectre chick, a gibbet spirit, uniquely broken,

unable to sift the topfreeze for specks of summer.

Wild Boar of New York

Sarah Hesketh

Remembering how Aristotle felt
metal-bound and hard to the throat,

the swart boar flirts the stoop.
Snaffling for trash, his ridgeback wig

stands stiff as a disguise.
He bides his time.

Haunted by the cuff of his feet
in sweet grass,

the burst flute of Aphrodite's calls
as he put her young god to the gore.

Gaddafi Gaddafi Gaddafi

Hannah Silva

I am not going to tell you my name Gaddafi but I am
going to tell you my age Gaddafi my age is ten
Gaddafi and I am going to tell you about a game
Gaddafi a game that I play Gaddafi I play with my
friends Gaddafi you can play it alone Gaddafi
or play it with friends Gaddafi. Go into a room
Gaddafi a room with strong walls
Gaddafi strong floor and strong ceiling
Gaddafi and choose a word Gaddafi not any word
Gaddafi but carefully Gaddafi you carefully choose
Gaddafi an immense word Gaddafi with immense meaning
Gaddafi with immense meaning to you Gaddafi
Gaddafi and with your friends Gaddafi all together
Gaddafi together you chant Gaddafi you chant that word
Gaddafi over and over Gaddafi Gaddafi over and over.
We chose a word Gaddafi we chose this word
'Gaddafi' we chant: Gaddafi Gaddafi Gaddafi
over and over Gaddafi Gaddafi Gaddafi
together Gaddafi Gaddifi Gaddafi
loudly Gaddafi Gaddafi Gaddafi all through
Gaddafi the night Gaddafi and through Gaddafi
the day Gaddafi the Gaddafi night the Gaddafi day:
Gaddafi Gaddafi Gaddafi. Other words might be quicker
Gaddafi but this word Gaddafi this word takes longer
Gaddafi Gaddafi. We stay in the room with

strong walls strong floor strong ceiling Gaddafi
Gaddafi for day after day after day Gaddafi
Gaddafi week after week after week Gaddafi
Gaddafi until Gaddafi at last Gaddafi one morning
Gaddafi one morning the word is the same
as all other words gaddafi gaddafi and we keep on
chanting gaddafi gaddafi gaddafi until the word loses
its meaning completely gaddafi and we keep on chanting
gaddafi gaddafi gaddafi we chant our way through this
loss of meaning until we become a gaddafi of horses
galloping: gaddafi gaddafi gaddafi.

Schwarzheide, 1986

Rob Stanton

You
only paint
what's there,
not what

is not: the
camp
has been
removed,

you paint
the trees;
the trees

have been
removed, you
paint the paint.

Rare Metallophytes

Tim Cresswell

Spring sandwort, alpine penny-cross,
mountain pansy: disaster lovers,
first on the scene of the misery
of ruptured earth, hanging on,
facing off, digging in. Coping
in the hinterlands of old lead mines.
Two months of cheerful, tufted
fuck-yous to the shafts and pylons left
by the dirt-encrusted hands and
steel-hard biceps of those who trucked off
the malleable metal for pistol shot,
roof flashing, batteries, radiation shields.

Kapoor's Temenos
Siddhartha Bose

I

Dog-whoof, spin-wharf,
>   gluttoned like a matrix. Curves of barbed wire.
>   Sky-shape tarot card.

>   Ear-cunt on arches.

Interstellar elongation, you surprise like a
>   spider, crawling out of that
>   goon-fog of a Middlesborough morning.

>   Stretched like a sleeping dinosaur. Temenos.

The air hints of smack, glass-crack, guillotined head-chops. My
friends like medieval scops
>   turntable tales of rise, decay, fall.
>   Tumble-town, this once was a steel-centre (Tenter-

hook me, heathen across oceans). Now, shut-factory tunes gloam
like ghosts (I see Hamlet's teeth edging from shroud of water).
Productive darkness.

Ravens appear, crib-caged, like babies. Pubs rake like skinheads.
College hipsters artfully pour their graces. And there, above all,

watching

> Temenos — dog-space divinity.
> (No more steel or ships. Or slaves.)

II

And you, mangled creator of space-art — mimic-man-cosma.
You left Bombay years ago (city of chatter-gods,
        mammon-fested monster.)

You journeyed from gray oceans, shifted imperially here,
        fashioned an accent out of breathing blood-clots. Peeled
        brown-skin from ivory-bone
        with ancient knives, to pupa yourself to a demi-god,
        poshed and polished.

Archetypal autocrat, scanning the fog of northern England, you
create mirrors o' yourself.

And there you are Anish bhai, locked with your visions on a foggy
Middlesborough morning —

        tentacled,

                cockroached,

                        infinite.

Honeymoon After Tikrit [i]

Emily Critchley

Won't you run with me now, past all the acting up & brushing off,
    & push me to float down *there* & there let me alone for good?
Won't you, when I'm *an insufficient woman,* point out the errors of
    my ways, the trail by which my false moves has everyone *be-*
    mused, & not ablaze?

& won't you cup me in yr hands & drink me on the sands, & send
    me on my way?
Won't you trash me in my talk & tie me to the mast, sail past me on
    a rock, split me at a word, defend me at the stake, & stake me as
    your claim, beat me when I'm lame, ride roughshod over when
    I'm good again,
& won't you always be so *good again,*
& won't you do *all* this
    for me, darling?

Won't you avoid me when I'm making love to someone else's
    company?
Won't you clip my wings & post them home, won't you melt my
    ways, then go out & buy yourself a telephone? Won't you live
    with me & be my love,
    & won't you harvest me & all the pleasures prove?
Won't you combine me with the gods above?
Won't you season me when I'm *sweet,* spring me when it's meet,
    chase me out of hiding for a treat. Or a song.

& won't you beat the devil out of me?
Won't you beat that ol' black devil off my back?
& won't you send me back where I belong?

Won't you turn out bad & say you're really good & shade in all
the colours in between?
& won't you do all this, & more for me, darling?
& won't you wink me for a trick, slink by me in a trice, & dice me
into salad, spill me for a shoulder (& good luck), & darling,
when you're *bolder*,
won't you risk me in a bet & double me or quit, & win me for
the rent, & fetter me unblent;
Won't you blow me like a joint & throw me to the wolves & hound
me like a dog & fill me with yr soothing words of love, fill my
head with soothing words of love *forever*?
Won't you do all this, & more, for me,
Won't you, darling?

Won't you screw me on the rack & rack me on the plate & plate me
to yr knife & knife me into afters?
& wont you, after all this, chase me into dust & rip me with yr teeth
& grind me into seed & crush my seed to earth & plant the earth
to loam & wash the loam to river & make the sun to shine &
plant the shine to grow & dust the grow to down & fill the down
to feather & weather up the best & rest me now to sleep & sleep
a thousand years with me & more?
Won't you do all *this* & *this* & so much more
for me, darling?

[i] Keith Tuma & Justin Katko, 'Holiday in Tikrit'

Such is the importance of shipwrecks

Steve Spence

Once the oil begins to wash ashore, damage will be
sudden and widespread. It's not the sex but the way
it's been commodified that's the problem. Now is the
time to take control of your career and gain the leading
edge. This is not the way to come to power, with
weapons in your hands. Much better to make your
approach on all-fours, yet they had small heads and
their brains were less than a third of the size of modern
human brains. Today we're looking at the effect of
volcanoes on our environment. In the hallway there
is a mirror which faithfully duplicates all appearances,
yet tall, silent horsemen patrol the roads. How do we
know that bats and birds developed wings independently?
Previous experience is not essential as training is provided.

Carbon
Melissa Lee-Houghton

I do not write to you, but of you,
because the paper that we write on
is our perishable skin.

Your photograph is inky and your face
chalked in by, honestly — honesty. You are
absolutely sure and absolutely not ready

to give. Your eyes see nothing of the dark
archipelago about your head, the lies
and the whispers surely love curtails —

that swim about your teeth and the years
that make your skin warm and then less warm.
All you know is that you need someone —

what a wedding band can do for the passage
of a girl who slips out of her knickers and into
her own despair, like there's nothing there.

Human Form

Oliver Dixon

Each morning we wake in a new
configuration: either
you've traded beds in a bumpy noctamble
and my first blink-cum-nuzzle
finds you shrunken, dream-morphed
from woman to boy;

or a nightmare's made him migrate
and upheave me,
and I come-to with feet exposed, arms
buckled in, Pluto and Tigger
my feral bedfellows,
Spiderman-lamp still on in the light.

Or even, he's somehow wriggled between
and spreadeagled,
entangling us in a cubist scrum:
we struggle into consciousness
like a many-limbed Lakshmi assuming
human form; or a ruffled, parodic

Trinity, momentarily conjoined.

Arvo Crash

Hannah Silva

He screams – she swears @ him.
There's Ø movN ndoors.
d c@ breathn on my gut.
A =o&o> zooms past,
a wmn on d bac S laffin.
d k9 S curled ^ on hs bed.
We're ll jst breathn. d 5-o siren
blaring as it pushes thru d traFK.
Calm dwn, dey sA 2 ea oder.
owtsd a CAB drivS past.
I'm nt movN. d tv S off
It's alw off n d daytime,
bt I'm nt calm. coz it's me –
d centA of ll dis. I'm d Ntrtamnt.
3 o'clock n d arvo, d tym I alw fall |-I.
IK I'm n my car. I read,
put dwn d b%k n DSapER.
I can't Xpln – my bod doesn't
seem lk my bod, it feels as f
4 hrs n sumtyms it S.
My lgz don't feel lk my lgz,
my arms don't feel lk my arms.
d animals r zzz.

Signs & Shivers
Iain Sinclair

BEACH SOCCER AXED OVER GUN VIOLENCE
FOX SAVAGES BABY TWINS
MOLEMAN TUNNELLER FOUND DEAD

DRIVING BAN DAD HANGED HIMSELF
SEX SPY 'CHARMED' GAZETTE SNAPPER

ECO-MUSLIM & FORMER PRESENTER
WIN GREAT TRIP TO SOUTH AFRICA
JUDGE STICKS KNIFE IN HACKNEY

QUEEN'S OFFICIAL BIRTHDAY
(SUBJECT TO CONFIRMATION)

WORLD'S TALLEST MAN
RETRIEVES OBJECT
FROM SICK DOLPHIN

FOX IN BLINDMAN'S BEDROOM
DEAF CAT IN MOTORWAY HORROR
LOST FRENCH TRUCKER KILLED OAP

EX-SOLDIER BEAT PAL INTO COMA
CUT CRIME WITH FEWER POLICE

FIREBUGS TORCH PARK AVIARY
A SHORT ROUTE TO A LONG BOX

U-TURN OVER GIANT BUNNY MURAL
CANNIBAL COPS FIND KILLER'S KIT

GIVE ME A CIGAR & RAISE THE SHADES

Kid
Abigail Oborne

Yeah so I
wiped coffee froth off my
wrists and watched
the cars and plastic bags
sifting past the window
heard the man say "I'm so excited
I'm just so excited about my fifteen
pound saving on my iPod-digi-nodal-modal-camera-lover"
and pick up his

blinking child. Listen kid,
I don't know what
kind of world has welcomed you
but still I sit here
cappuccino fed and biscotti wrapper
dead shell. Still the buses, the buses
coming fast, three in each direction
but here's a solid silence between you

and me, the best thing between all my crappy jobs
and angry days.
"It's you and me babe,"
I heard you say at seven thirty
this morning over the hairdryer and the
clang of my eyes

so here's today and it's you and
me babe/mate/brother/sister/dad/God.

Richard Branson
Ross Sutherland

My love, I feel like this print of Rothko.
I am small and glassy and I want to impress you,
even if it means murdering one of your work colleagues.

You think if you stare long enough at your noodles
you'll see the combination to the safe.
I don't have the heart to tell you the truth.

Even the elephant on the 20 Rand note
you gave me for good luck back in 2009
will end up spent in the end.

You adjust my tie and I grow a little older.

On cold hungover days, the white sun follows us
through Jesus Green to the Carphone Warehouse.

Shrek watches from the electrical shop across the street;
seven Shreks, running in parallel across a burning rope bridge.
It's impossible to root for any of them.

A millionaire's hairstyle
is trapped in the era they first made their money.

The air turns green above the poles of the Earth.

Poem in Which You Ask How You Can Tell Real Pearls from High Quality Fakes

Claire Trévien

Ultimately does it matter if the pearls are real or not?
The earth is a pearl, blinding and flawed,
nestled inside the mollusc of the milky way.
Do you prefer your pearls cultured in the art
of oology, or simply coated in fish scales?
Check if you must, where would I start to look
for your realness? By prodding your cheeks,
perhaps, holding your eyes against the light,
taking a sample of your speech for testing,
cataloguing evidence of feeling in your tone.

from Count from Zero to One Hundred
Alan Cunningham

What would it be like to be in a strong land, you think, as you lie down and try to sleep, try to stop that heart pounding, a land where people are strong, fit, healthy and whole, and you would pretend that you are like them all, everyone would pretend, but you are not, you realise, you simply want an approving gaze, and you are not even sure you want that.

•

As you lie there you think about what it is you feel you have to say, why you feel you cannot say it in the company of others, why you fear being known, knowing that you are known, knowing that it is all so obvious, fearing the breakdown of your body, the gaze of the eye that sees you and knows you and:

she did not know you, she saw you as she wanted to, as you presented yourself to her, which was what you believed she wanted, what all want, but yet you could be comfortable around her, it was not that, it was her fear of the gaze of others, that was what caused you to decay, her fear — you saw it — of being completely herself and then you realise that this, this fear, is what you fear of others, because you cannot understand it:

you know exactly what you are, what you are capable of, what you are incapable of and that gives you grace, you do not feel the need to be otherwise, you have no choice, it can all be seen, others can hide too easily, their bodies allow them that, and that makes you fearful, that they cannot really be seen, that they will change what is in the mind, but their bodies will stay the same, beautiful, capable of convincing you, you cannot convince with your body, it is all to easy to see that you are broken down, a wreck, incapable of the poise you always affect.

•

As you begin to feel that you are sleeping, you think: in that strong land your mind is seen as a deformity, but your mind is clear, you are not lying and your body can never be untruthful.

Long Letter; Short Farewell

SJ Fowler & Sam Riviere

Date: Mon, 28 Jan 2013 17:24:04 +0000
From: █████████████████████████
Subject: collaboration for enemies
To: ███████████████████████

dear sam,

hope you're good. no worries if its not of interest but perhaps youve seen iv got a book of collaborations coming out with penned later in the year, ive mentioned it once or twice about maybe doing a short collaboration for it. how about an exchange of ██████ poems? you can pick a theme, or just abstractions, we could xchang ███████ ██████ or something.

very best
steve

From: Samuel Riviere ██████████████

██████████████████████████

Sent: Tuesday, 29 January 2013, 17:44
Subject: RE: collaboration for enemies 2/?

Dear S,

– now we all live in the same anthologies, friends at last, a suspicious
calm descends. The cause of wars is boredom… Who feels on edge?
And who'd be *your* enemy, really? We should make some new ones.
I'll admit that your use of the lower case intrigues me… I reserve
it usually for enquiries from editors and agents: disrupt them with
the lower case, no punctuation. Who adapts, etc — in even these
transactions syntax feels power struggle. Your note's informality,
its deadly *approachability*, is, I'm afraid, partly to blame for…*this*
— I'm *italicising*, in an email! *My* italics. Oh Steven, sometimes I
worry about our generation…I mean I wonder, what will become
of us? What will we be called? Are we even part of 'our' generation,
anyway? Most of the time I'm vaguely shamed by it — its music,
its shitty films. I mean, I hate the Oscars. I'm a mainstream kid. I
read a pome in one of those Oxford mags, it was a nice little pome
like Ted Hughes without the animals. (Those tears will not travel.)
We should refuse participation — absolutely; and in the remit of the
pome an arena be opened where I can air my grievances, legit. The
mainstream is the real alternative because it is so mainstream, it goes
around like a bad joke. Today the Google car went past, I waved. I
was out to buy some eggs. It rained, it didn't rain, I mean come on. If
we must joust, remember please that I abhor violence in all its forms,
metaphorical or otherwise. I have nothing to say to my friends (we
all agree) so enemies are the best ones. If only Americans weren't so
loud about their feelings, eh? The One Where Joey and Ross Discuss

Poetry. Overall I *liked* your question, the whole vibe and vector of it. I'm upset to not have been plagiarised yet. Resentment is the only thing holding poetry together. We need our Oceania. The biogs are too long and are not relevant to the publication.

Your enemy,

Sam

Date: Tue, 29 Jan 2013 23:12:57 +0000
From: ████████████████████
Subject: Re: collaboration for enemies 2/?
To: ████████████████████

Dear S,

my problems are similar to yours but shifted schematically by a few degrees purely through the un / fortunate reality of chance, as it relates to beginnings, as in enough to know the difference between a real and imagined problem but not enough to have an excuse to be something other than feeling generally well in an attempt to surround myself with a something which is akin to love (or is actually that), which is hard to say, thanks, in part, to the pomes you refer too. and that is an idea of love which is based on knowing what it's opposite is. which is a good way, i have found, to approach concerns like 'generations', 'poetry', 'approachability', as well as love. by the way, are we not friends enough yet for lower case? I've met your ████ and you've met mine (as if we'd be married at our age, generationally), and lest you forget, I've been to where you live. certainly we're friends enough that I might ask you to be part of enemies, somehow, even if obituaries or ▮▮▮▮ poems or whatever isn't quite right for you. there is a significant cache around you at the moment because of your book with faber, you have to suspect i might be attempting to bungle hump your coverage into my book somehow. is it all an exchange perhaps? that would be a naive reading of human interaction (where there is warmth to be found, occasionally often) by the kind of arsehole i often have to deal with who would consider themselves revolutionary and thus not capable of the most basic self awareness. do you know what im getting at? that people assume their cynicism is the final destination, when in many ways, it is the first stop? a token of something to show my in / sincerity - no violence. & I shall, at a later date, plagiarise you with great care / ease.

your enemy
steve

The Method

Rob Stanton

We'll never know that unbelievable
head, those outstanding eyes. The trunk
stills shines, but more like a subdued candelabrum
reflecting on its own reluctant – if

staggering – power. Why else would we
be riveted to that impressive chest? Why else
notice that chuckle spread down tensing abs
to a barely-there but still productive groin?

Take that and all you're left with is a slab
of mutilated stone – defeated, slumped – not
glistening like a predator's subtle fur, nor

diffusing light of stars' intensity. There's
not a single part of it that does not
see your life. You must change.

Our Glasnost Love
Chris McCabe

Back in the Häagen-Dazs we made Bang & Olufsen plans
our mercantile enemies had Staropramen breathe
— their plastic strips cashed red districts of glass —
our praline fingers melted Volkswagen buckles,
spread a flood your Scandinavian fishnets could not
hold, we let it age our Mercedes-Benz hair
more silver than a customs' penknife
in the top pocket of the highest ranking M.E.P.
his briefcase stocked with our pillowcase croissants,
anchovies shocked black your trois-fromage bloom
— for love j'ai faim, j'ai faim for your breasts —
our monoprix fix axed by Teutonic crows
doppelgänging time down the strasse of our twenties,
Heloise & Abelard stumped to page & stage more dunkel
than any Erdinger pin-flaxed with onyx blackout
down La Rambla, the slot-erotics of The Wall,
hunched for names in le pleuvoir of Père Lachaise,
all condensed — condensed for the quick — I've come
destination, this once I've arrived — your autobahn eyes

from NOT AN ESSAY
Heather Phillipson

In the nightclub, people salute biology through pressed-up bodies. Presumably in search of high-voltage incidents, people — faces tacked on, air dark as the brutish — wait to be jump-started. Crumbs in a see-thru freezer-bag, we move forwards, sideways, bang hearts together, grittily. Rolling down-stage, holding digitized money. Spending it. In the nicest way possible, make it a Gin & Slimline Tonic. A G&T is a human moment. Although we feel elated, we wouldn't say we feel cosy in our new trousers. We see uncertainty around the edges. We are like a person who says *I live right in the middle of town* then catches a bus home to the fringes.

Perhaps Other Reasons

Emily Critchley

That cat gut you've inserted through my mouth,
It travels down my spine, fires & tugs
With every movement, 'specially in my loins ~
It is the fruit of all seasons; a bird
For every journey ~ on each vital organ.
It has a tension you wouldn't believe, a sssssspiccato
Belonging to the '60s. I mean the 1660s.
It is a little heinous corpus when I
Bend under. If you squared it with the up stroke,
You might smooth things over for a while ~
At least till I return to some other
Decimated breeding ground where the mood
Is fertile & the land more perchy.
Such times are tough, & I get easily strung out.
Also, I find with every era that goes by
This little throat gets less & less tuneful /
More grating to the ear. I hate to catch you
On~the~wing for such discussions.
& there are perhaps other reasons why
It's not the best idea

Gists and Piths

George Ttoouli

for ST

A Japanese student in America, on being asked the difference
between prose and poetry, said: Poetry consists of gists and piths.
—Ezra Pound

No, I mean the sun
        cannot, the colour of orange
                peel does not or the trees
        repay us with a wave, just like —
and so if the, you know, mistranslates
        between the green and grey,
                olive husks/body rind/pre-crematoria —
        the happy/glad oil cannot
and crazy/dead husks do not,
        et cetera, and this knot in my pen —
                like day lancing the ignorant boil —
        like love being what someone said
in a poem not so long ago, Yes?
        I would rather cook my eyes
                than not see you again!
        I mean that the sun cannot be
the colour of sand under a rock, Yes?
        Crabs! No, onions! Crying
                before you've reached the heart of,
        caramelised/flavour-changed, world
in a different — you
        on my tongue — could the tang/sweet
                melt or bite into an apple/onion, Yes?
        That the onion layers remind me

of how the trees will drop
　　　olives and husks will crack under our sideways
　　　　　　and so life is a fried orange, Yes?
　　　And if you and I were crabs/husks
and had no oil/tongues
　　　to cremate our skins
　　　　　　in the passion of our frying
　　　then our love would be
long as the sun —
　　　and as long as
　　　　　　the sun — illogical.

Charismatic Megafauna
Tamsin Kendrick

I have travelled far in Japanese silk slippers;
the geishas broke my feet. I wear a fedora hat
for mystery solving and brandy drinking,
a rag tag of skirts, leggings, a naked knee,
a burn on my thigh, a blood dream.

Towards the Temple I open.

Gold rings on three of my fingers, for bartering,
for proof I am the child of the electric priest
and his red-headed Jew, full of breast,
whom he loved and rescued from the suburbs

but refused to sing to. Introverted,

he paces the roof garden and mumbles
strange languages beneath a sky that loves him.
His footsteps pop with new life. The trees harmonise.

This is where I began, nestled small in the pelvis
of an acoustic. Chords vibrating bones,
pickings trembling skin. Daddy is muci

floating through the bedroom ceiling, Daddy is love,
incense, promises tied to red bows. Daddy is my passage

through the avenue of vines, the gatekeeper to ths synagogue.
He holds my hand as towards the Temple we open.

Things To Do Before You Leave Town

Ross Sutherland

Attempt to tessellate everything
you've never wanted
and ever known.
Cut the phone. Bleed the radiators.
Cancel bills, subscriptions, friendships.
Tell Steve to go fuck himself.
Introduce your creditors
to those who owe you favours.
Find something creepy
to offer your neighbours:
a small key, a stethoscope.
I thought you might like this…
Use 'mate' like a newsagent.
Meet Claire, but fail to notice.
Do not set out a timetable of withdrawal.
Do not return your library books.
Do not go back for your coat.
Do not hard-talk the homeless.
Do not stare longingly up at the clock tower.
Stop taking yourself so seriously.
This is your final warning.
Put on 'Uptown Top Rankin'
in the first pub you drank in.
Try to enjoy the boredom.
If you can, spread it around.

Come midnight, throw
a glow-in-the-dark frisbee
off the highest point in town.

Coney Island Cribs
Sarah Hesketh

The Electric Michaelangelo's
given up carving arms next door.

The haruspicator's entrails
have boiled themselves to soup.

If you want to find Captain Bonavita
when he's done

repeating early Baudelaire
to his lions,

then sneak past the generator's burr
and take a peek

at these faces pulled from waists too soon,
these improbable fruits

whose stuttered mewlings
have got the Fat Lady sitting

and knitting snug booties,
prompted Lobster Boy

and the Invisible Man

to spend less time than they might

over chess. A million lightbulbs
hum loosely around the boardwalk fence.

They taunt the moon. Her blank particulars
shunt the tide in protest.

A Volta for the Sonnet as a Drag Queen

Sophie Mayer

1

The sonnet's a drag, and girl, it knows: sticks its
falsies, lines up its lashes. Lamé, lurex, tits
aglitter, it plays the crying game. To be real.
To see how it makes you, makes you, makes you feel,

to be real. The sonnet's a pose. Vogue. Let your
body be told what (not) to do. To the letter,
in its frame. Again, again. Limbs aglow/akimbo
if enjambed: the stance, the torch, the blow

that's always coming. The twist, you know it.
What's underneath the hood. In her panties.
What reveals, conceals. What (split) ends. Take no shit,
darling, that's the deal. The impossible with ease.

2

This ooze is us: the tilting city of us visible
in its shunting, in its melismas. Who cast us
in clear resin, jarred us, until here we are: dis
played. Mutated to meet the needs of
a poisoned world. Gill to gill we dance,
my crotch pressed up between your prostheses,
the necklace of my tumours tangled
in your iridescent locks. What prophetic tango
our skin speaks, our nifty six fingertips (light
at loom or touchscreen, equally). My squally
darling, my freak show embryo: we will drag
ourselves over the slivers. Spike our cha-cha heels
with them, rim each orifice with shards of glass.
And glitter. And glitter. And. And glitter.

Church Hill
David Caddy

I have been there and I am
impatient to return. Silent
and motionless it is surrounded.
With each step we get closer.

I can speak of this virus
that loiters by the wire fence,
of the prattle that passes for dialogue,
the wind that lashes a man's throat.

I propose to you a hill.
In the woods rooks call attention
to our presence.
Our bodies are full of expectation.

It hurts to live the way we do
wanting so much
unable to cope with this longing
unwilling to wait.

The landscape we love grows dark
so easily. Turning back we feel
the need to stop and linger.
We move. Stop. Are soon gone.

Spring-Summer Collection
James Wilkes

This is ethereal cannonade. This season's acoustics: snare pops, crunch and yodelling. Correspondents shift uncomfortably and thumb their paperbacks until: autonomous movement, first model out walking fast and radical. For inspiration, think the legs, tucked and extended, in old horse paintings, so her canter swings sufficiently the hem. No coincidence that Technotronic's *Pump up the Jam* reverberates the glittered plywood. Released in 1989: Solidarność legalised, the Wall in ruins, the Velvet Revolution. Surely this Belgian new beat classic thus picks out choreography to plead a European pose contra neo-lib hegemony? – Yes but what about her clothes?

    iridescent
    buttons

    pleats (still
    bounces
.   with
    resid-
    ual
    swing)

    navy &
    ochre trim

    a nice
    hat

Correspondents embellish as she turns, and her double emerges from the wings. Significant details: the vestigially protective aspect of the collar; the soft flare and gather of material at the spine; how light can be coddled to do this; the mauve gloves; the paisley. Chiasmus as they pass, the swaying balance of retreating night, advanced severity in pin-stripe. Couture tilts unpredictably against the bias, a surface happy under strip lights or a cavernous pigeon sky. The covering is slashed, reveals an undercover – orange, louche, and redolent of cooking. Calm, she stops,

    bearing all
    the lines
    of business

    the return
    of figures
    ruptures

    soft power
    of allure
    haunted

for an audience. Her footfalls crash with sudden loss of faith, the weathered end of wealth her economic turndowns at the heel. Transparent baubles bursting in her tress, and veined like estuary surfaces her jacket's sea-glass cincture plays opaque; she saunters off. Makes room for tartan whimsy, repurposed panels stiffly cut and held with cleats and ribboning. Nothing says informal economy like tarpaulin, it's almost like the plastic weave itself is aching to enfold around her as a bag:

upholstery
staples

glint and
hold her

a short
-term
contract
with cerise
dungarees

as the DJ hides the seams and house's corridors extend their vanishing colonially through this. And OMG, a shawl is flicked around her shoulders like they're knocked off Fendi bag and run before the carabinieri crack some skulls, enamelled lemon lacquer on her thinly ridged and stacked-up heels, she wavers and she vanishes before our eyes. Silence, silenzio, and the next look marries the sea, which is a kind of people, an irregular unpleated stance. What supple canes maintain her new and ample blue as field of crumpled zones around the working legs, whilst at the apex of disturbed habiliment parades a precious manikin. Awkward to hold, a delightful clutch,

slipping
shearing

violet torn
white flecks

tectonic
round the

knees, elbows
worn to a

collage of
movement

and display
and topped

with a
jesus handbag

She executes a volta: collective gasp, her back is bare and tattooed
with a pensive St. Jerome, big and red and leonine in Ray-Bans
and outrageous headgear. She offers up a beatific pose, balancing
the pedals expertly on kitsch and gas. We need some more like her.
Now listen: I know a fabric where the onion is raw like silk – but
shop talk is as short as breath. A petrol hairpiece keeping pace with
scintillating sugar-cane cement hits town, a single hairpinned length
unrolling,

of chance
ikebana, like

Wolfgang
Tillmans

composed
the jumpsuit

from tea-water
window light

& grains
of Super 8

that smear the stage. It's all going turmeric until the techies intervene,
slap the filters on above and turn the whole thing coral. It must be
for the sailor's cap, or possibly the pea-green coat which hangs like
calving ice – and falls as the DJ mashes *Tainted Love* with a rare
translation of Raymond Carver into French. A mellow sonority of
rum and shag: *soudain, je trouve un nouveau chemin à la cataracte*, though
correspondents note the laser-cut and porous bangles effervescing
from ankles up to thighs: well.

A cropped
fawn
ziggurat

& palettes
there
to be

broken,

fuchsia
malachite

& bolts of
camel

would say that wouldn't it? But thanks to penicillin, skirts are floatier now we're not afraid of catching death and forced to fend it off with horsehair, cummerbunds and oil. The merest updraft billows out the carefree voiles, the kicked-up plumes and bronze and open canopies. The scent unwraps like complex chestnut chandeliers. So ciao to caution, ciao to solitude, from here you balance like you mean it, a one-shouldered cut against a dazzling azalea. Sophisticated *and* populist: with detailing so asymmetric, how can it go wrong?

Time Permitting

Oliver Dixon

Summer has come to this: the sky invaded
by parachutes of cloud; abrupt random downpours
no sooner sheltered from than giving way

to precarious outbursts of sun. All season
has seemed this waiting for the season
to begin: waiting for the weather to include

us in its plans, or settle into patterns
no sooner framed than autumn will abridge
them, hauling down the coloured tents of summer,

moving on. It will come to this: swallows
giving way to the veering pipistrelle;
the ash-tree going to pieces on the lawn.

Scop
Meghan Purvis

If it's stories of S<small>IGEMUND</small> you're wanting,
I can tell you right now, we don't have enough ink.
I could speak until nightfall
with you scribbling away, and you wouldn't know

the half of it. Not that you'd believe me anyway —
between him and his nephew F<small>ITELA</small>,
they got into enough battles to fill a history book,
laid eyes on enough wonders to fill a dictionary.

But his most famous deed — the one they still shout for
when the hall runs out of beer and over with boasting —
he did alone, under the earth. That was when he killed the dragon,
impaling it on a sword standing deep in the rockwall.

He earned the treasure he carried out of that place;
a ship low-waterlined with gold and bright rings,
the serpent burning behind him.
He was the champion we had prayed for,

growing stronger after H<small>EREMOD</small>'s weakening,
when he was betrayed to the giants and killed.
That one brought sorrow to his people, grief to his thanes,
though only I am left to remember it now.

We had looked to our prince to save us, to protect
his land and his people. BEOWULF is loved by all who know him,
but Heremod's hand fell heavy; his eye passed over
in a darkness that would not lift. I will not pass his story on.

On Raymond's Bike

Susie Gordon

Sitting on the bus beside my aunt
we crossed the wide dry veldt of Blackheath
and she told me how my father and she
would high-tail over it on Raymond's motorbike
back when the days seemed longer.

Every street in those postcodes
is x-marked with my aunt's rememberings -
the willow tree in Bellingham, the backyards
and the boulevards, people's pasts and life-spans
spreading in the messy deal of slippy neon photos
splayed out on the carpet or twitching on old ciné -
things that went before us, made us.

All of us, as halves
of selves, twists of DNA, must have been
five times each around the world, so I -
as demi-curl of chromosome - have buzzed
over Blackheath Common on Raymond's bike
as the evening settled, and the sun embered
down over Woolwich.

Beautiful Girls

Melissa Lee-Houghton

In our graves we are all
beautiful girls. Our skin
is falling away like the tide.
Our bones are
long and slender,
all inhibitions gone. We're
lovely in the mud
that fit boys have dug
for a council wage,
not knowing how beautiful
we lay there
like honeymoon brides
anticipating sex,
not expecting death —
serene as pawns and queens
and home in ourselves
forever.

Animal City
Siddhartha Bose

I

Twin-bride of my ten-head home, I
  watch you closely from the
  cross of scorched lands, rubble of sea-foam,
    fire of snake-tongue.

Grand and pungent in act, I long to write you an epic
  worthy of our ancient tales.

For now, these
  bites will do, as I
  chrome myself round your lingo,
scalding my brow with your
  tears of grime, shame, bigtalk wealth.

I gender you in full-on
  curry angrezi, with
  patois political, image transcontinental.

II

Close on nine years you
  be my multiverse, *Bombay meri jaan.*

Now me your bastard
        ratshipper, who you coldthaw by turns,
        breaking limbs, tossing one by one after
            chop-'n'-changing me to your

dogs that bark the
        rounds of Kala Ghoda.

Me you fat in slums stomach-lining
        Chatrapati Shivaji International Airport,

me you snatch like the sea necklace by
        Marine Drive,

me you step underfoot towards the
        mosque that grows from the sea, by
        Hajiali, breakin me into the south.

Me you bleed on treetops that crown Siddhi-Vinayak,
        pole-vaulting through cricket parks, churchbells,
                                                lion in Sion.

Me you gorge in dark Bandra sounds,
        with India electronica, the asli bhangra.

Me you lick in clamour bars of Juhu,
        palm trees and pork by the sea-view.

Me you sweat in pav bhaji streets, pani-puri

gag, vada pao itch.

Me you wet in tobacco nights, incense from
        Nigerian peddlars in Colaba, fevered.

III

You are my crude health, the
        crass in my conscience.

(Once, one of your statue saints called out, at the
        curve of Mahim, as the smog of sun
        cut through canopy trees in
cockroach antennae: 'Life's an echo. You get back what you give.')

I remember too much. I insurrect. I thaw.

IV

Recalling me pulling out ear-wax,
        galling me, heavy and brown and long like rat shit, by
        Cuffe Parade at the ballpoint pen-tip of South Bombay.
        I see through large French windows, fishing-nets, seasalt.
                wood smells like horse-hide.

On the bus back to Versova, home from school, my
        Math teacher yells me bout

them Goan sausages, how spicy they be, my
mother would like them.

My first love, Aditi, in the school closeby
Amitabh Bachchan's house. I thought her an
androgyne, as in my child-wet dreams, we'd
fly over electric grass, whitelight in Andheri.

But no no, I tell it straight, one
image stark stays, genuine.

V

We stop on Linking Road in days when Fiats
clogged the shape of traffic towards Mahim Causeway.

Long before the whip of olive bars, mojo melts, too school for cool
drawl-mocking
Mumbaikars, sultry and bangled Bandra girls.

No, back in the '80s, a few years before I
played football with a bat-blind cancered grandfather, my
mother 'n' me stop at the corner where Waterfield Road
spills.

(Nearby, Maa liked the cottage-cheese shop.)

As we wait for the green light, a

sadhu six-footed walks to my openaired window,
      dreads-matted, beard in forest, saffron-covered with
            hint of charcoal, fume, lavender.

Him have a sleek, spotted,
      jazz-patterned python wrapped round his
      upper torso, fitted perfect like a bride's sari. The snakehead
                                    juts out
      in a slither above his locks.

He stretches them crow hands, pigeon nails,
      towards me, eyes fired, jaundiced yellow.

I recoil, screaming. A
      hijra on the street-divider claps his hands,
      clacks like a witch. Light greens, cars cough, cop
            blinks. Maa shakes.

            VI

Them surrealists were hacks, term-tablers, scabs on a
            tired, southern Europe.

They never knew you, O animal city, where a thousand gods
            jostle like men hanging outta late-evening suburban trains,
            rowdy, brutal, bleeding.

Now some call you Mayanagri, but in me —

traitor—you be the slick oil, the
steel breath, the becoming cancerous starshape of a
      fresh from sleep, proud,
                seething century.

'Mayanagri' translates, popularly, as 'city of dreams'. A 'hijra' is a eunuch.

from Holophin
Luke Kennard

After an hour on the production line (working on colour today, a simple job topping up tiny funnels with pigments, adhesives and glitters – *Hand painted: no two Holophins are alike, outside or in!* – and making sure the automated painting system runs smoothly) Hatsuka and Max have English with Mr Harris. They are on friendly terms with Harris, and frequently drink tea in his office. He smells like a second hand bookshop and claims to hate Holophins, which is as it should be. *A computer, a confidant, a carer, a friend!* Mr Harris is nicknamed Mr Harassed – a pun on the ludicrous English pronunciation – because he is English and has a put-upon air.

Max takes an extra-credit module with Harris called *Post-Industrial Dystopias*. Like the whole Arts Faculty, Harris uses paper in his lessons, and students are required to take off their Holophins. They stick them to their exercise books. This is a peculiarity of the Takin International School and the subject of no little controversy. They keep their own sustainable forest in the South of the country, which doubles as a theme park.

In today's lesson Mr Harris confesses to the class that the eleven poets they have studied for the last three months were all made up. By him.

The class is too shocked to murmur disconsolately. Hatsuka is particularly upset: the unique phrasings of Anya Kochinskaya, 20th century Belarusian dissident murdered in a camera shop, particularly touched her heart. She feels like she has spent a month comforting a friend whose illness turns out to be bogus.

'I apologise for the deception, of course,' says Harris. 'But it was in the service of an important point re. the credibility of the first Holophin poet, whose work we move onto later today. Now, I fabricated the life stories, bibliographies and major works of all eleven poets. It took me about a year. Not one of them is real. Does it matter? Of course not.' Several hands go up. Harris ignores them. 'Culturally speaking, after World War Two we lost our nerve altogether. The show was over, you might say, and since then Western culture has been a late revue for the people with no good reason to go home. The last two generations, me and you, we're not even that. We're an open-mic session tailing off into the remaining drunks in the theatre bar who can't take a hint, and we all think we're artists.'

'Sir,' says Max. His hand has been up for some time.

'Literature is a programme like anything else,' says Mr Harris. 'Now, you can say what you like about Holophins, but they have an innocent belief in their own talent. And this gives them the potential to produce some beautiful literature. You'll notice I say "innocent" and not "naïve".' Mr Harris writes NAÏVE and INNOCENT on the board, with some hopeful spider-legs shooting out. 'Who'd care to parse these terms?'

Silence. Adalmut raises her hand.

'Naïvety is, like, an excuse,' she says. 'Like you've done something stupid which needs to be justified.'

From the row behind, Hatsuka looks at Adalmut's slender neck, like the magnified curve of a stamen. Her hair is up in a bun to show off her gold teardrop earrings. Adalmut answers every question as if you had asked her how she was feeling. Hatsuka almost envies it. Is Adalmut naïve or innocent?

'Great, that's great,' says Mr Harris. 'Anyone else?'

'To be innocent is to be uncorrupted by negative influence,' says Hatsuka. 'To be naïve is to lack experience. Critically, it is to lack the insight to *realise* that you lack experience. We were naïve to trust you, for instance.'

'Good,' says Mr Harris, thinking better of the brainstorm and wiping the board clean. He is, in so many ways, a total trainwreck as a teacher, which is why Hatsuka likes him. It is our weaknesses which decide the nature of our virtues. Our faults which we can least afford to lose. A system which recognises this is Hatsuka's dream. Codename St Paul, or something.

'The Holophins have "read" everything,' says Mr Harris, taking a swig of coffee from his Holophin mug. 'Everything. More than a human could read in a hundred lifetimes. But they are *innocent* of ambition, uncowed by those they might consider their betters. They have no jealousy or ulterior motive. They share our will to create, hysterically they share that, but eschew our wanton ambition.'

'But that's what makes us human,' says Max.

The Holophins should have flaws, is the feeling among the upper echelons. Wabi. Nothing lasts, nothing is finished and nothing is perfect. They are currently appointing a professor to teach Wabi-Sabi. This is why Hatsuka and Max are working on Status Anxiety. Mr Harris clearly hasn't been informed, but then why would they tell him? He's been teaching English here for twelve years and is still an adjunct.

'A good note,' he says to Max, 'on which to introduce Holophin #6406348364's poetry.' [See Appendix 1, 'Dolphin With a Time Machine' reprinted with kind permission from Holophin #6406348364's fourth collection.] [N.B.: RETRACTED.]

Mr Harris delivers his photocopied handouts by hand. He literally hands them out. Most Arts teachers leave them in a pile and you pick them up as you go in. If you forget, you get up and collect one. Harris's gesture would be agreeable if it didn't take up five minutes of a forty minute lesson.

Dr Wha

James Robertson

Wha's Doctor Wha? Wha better kens nor he
that jouks the yetts and rides the birlin wheels
o time and space, shape-shiftin as he reels
through endless versions o reality?
But dis he ken himsel? Weel, mibbe sae,
yet wha's tae ken gin aw that's kent by Wha
maks mair or less or better sense ava
nor whit we ithers ken, or think we dae?
The universe is fou o parallels:
wha's like us? Hunners? Thoosans? We oorsels
micht be mere glisks o life-forms yet tae be.
Whit's real? Whaur's here? When's noo? Wha's quick or deid?
Wha's jist a thochtie in anither's heid?
Wha's Doctor Wha? Wha better kens nor he?

Communion

Claire Trévien

The weather's gained weight,
sags its pebbled belly against the tips
of the city's horns.

I've slumped, waiting for it to decide,
grotesque piñata, whether to burst
or rapture itself away.

The world has ended, or, at least,
most people have. I am no Avenger:
I have found wine spared

in collapsed cellars; it tastes of hills
now plucked out of reach. Grapes
have been crushed, made to sour

for my pleasure. Unwaged fingers
now mingle with the vines
while the wine runs down my throat.

Broken bottles, broken sky: red rain
heaves out of the cracked world.
I open my mouth for communion.

On Unpredictable Weather Conditions
Heather Phillipson

Once, in Ohio, I faced a tornado.
The sky was a dirty curtain, and then rainfall -
a bit like tonight in East London on your futon
with the weather at the window and you asleep to my left,
only there I was alone and calmer.

This pillowcase, left by your ex, has a nice pattern.
I wish it didn't. Perhaps she had significance
and a fabulous lilac jacket. I want to stay longer
under your winter duvet. One day
I'd like to put your paper clips in order.

See how I take the side furthest from the door?
In the wind in the night in a booming Columbus suburb
in the eye of meaningless panic most of life ran for cover.
But here, mad with trepidation, I run towards your cyclone.

boats

Michael Egan

late evening the harbour is speckled with boats
running to the water's edge as the tide grew
we saw them unending ships with gaping beast heads

an image too strong is the rod bound with the blade
now grown they have awareness of its purpose
still they toy with the bundle like children

in the lack is his diagram loose and random
sprawling towards realism never given
could not last my beautiful cell full of energy

and we have not had such a clear night
since the post office closed
only a fever delirium not a definite end.

Heaven

Melissa Lee-Houghton

Heaven is the place between the sky and the planets.
You have to soar through the clouds to reach it.
You go there if you have a personality disorder
or learning disability, or if you made all three appointments
in a row. The drugs give you extra lift
as you go. When you get there
you can be invisible. You spend most of your life
that way — it's a comfort. Only now you never cry
and you don't need anyone to watch you cling to life.
Heaven is the place where we spend eternity, amazed
that life has to happen at all;
the place where we are unnoticed and learn to sing songs
backwards and spell out names in languages
no-one uses. We don't have to worry about our insides
or being mistaken for someone else. Being forgotten
is beautiful. Being forgotten has not always been beautiful.

(Re.vision)
Emily Critchley

That is how progress. That is wine settling
toward taking its place. The vast limping, throat at your tiller.
Land where future machinery palls irrespective
and at the side of major authority brains perpetual delirium.

That is not what I meant progress. I who argued for I to extinguish
the sun in midst of zinc, etymologize hardly, print out manically
all the marginalized errors. Mine not yours / hers / his / its, etc.

Your supporters on crutches, your cerebral cortex speeding
on floating hammers. Remove that masses and come sit.
I want your title, address, wristwatch & everything else
you see tensely. A sideline's possible. Then mounting objectives
take optimism, strangulate, it is all on outside.

Incorrigibly Plural

Simon Barraclough

The network froze from the wrong kind of snow
so they carved up the sky and franchised the clouds
and tempests of tenders, flurries of offers,
brochures in blizzards descended upon us.

Heavenly companies, flocculent liveries:

   Cumulo-Western-Coast

      Capital-Nimbo-Link

         Cirro-Southeastern-Star

gliding like bullet points into the stratosphere,
each with a strategy, mandate, philosophy,
swelling the market of snowflake delivery.

Our cloud is committed to cutting-edge crystals.
The eye of our storm places **you** *at the centre.*
Our flakes have been voted the least identical;
from vapour to whiteout they were the most punctual
over the Christmas and New Year period.

In the last fiscal year we shifted a zillion
units of snow, including the state-of-the-art 'Bendilo':

dendrical with a hexagonal interlock,
leading to more compact drifts and an authentic
lacing around a bow window. And each metric tonne
of precipitate fun comes with a free scarf
and a kit for the kiddies of snowman accessories:
a carrot, some coal from a genuine steam train,
a pipe, a fedora, a handful of pebbles
for studding a smile into his blank face
like the one we're committed by charter to place
upon yours.

Poem Looked Up on Google Streetview
Ross Sutherland

Two girls in sympathetic postures and winter coats
are swapping stories about ~~Northern cities~~ ~~granddads~~
~~impractical music stands~~ psychoholography,
sat on the cold stone steps of ~~a chiropodist's~~ an editing suite.

Nearby, a ~~cycle courier~~ process server
stares at ~~a sticker book of barcodes~~
~~a holiday spread in the Express~~ a terrible sandwich
with a look that is unreservedly ~~content~~ sinister ~~both~~.

Meanwhile, some fifty-five miles east and three years later,
I am sitting here anchored off the coast of this story,
trying to imagine how this gripping yarn will end,
or even (let's be honest) how it intends to begin.

Software has automatically removed the identities
of the hundred people that led our characters
up to this moment, their faces blotted out
with bits of British sky.

Across the street, a man with the haircut of a pianist
walks purposefully towards Dean Street,
yet try to follow him and you join another timeline.
The city resets at the crossroads, jumps back to 6am,

leaving nothing on the road but chalked instructions
for yesterday's ~~Climate Camp~~ ~~Pro-Tibet protest~~
rally against Sir Ian Blair
already fading back into the tarmac.

These empty moments
are often the most complicated,
where the thousandth analogy for London breaks down.
London is not a broken river, nor a waterlogged mirror,

nor an ageing, racist, colour-blind boxer.
If we assigned a metaphor to it, we'd just end up
talking about something else.

Wet Paint says the sign on the railings,
which is the closest we're going to get to prophecy —
everything here is still waiting to dry,
for the artist to return from his long lunch

and sketch that central character into the frame,
some camped-up London duke or pinstriped Beefeater.
Then again, perhaps the reason that we cannot see the hero
is because we are already possessing its body:

the Google Car itself, with its horrible insect eye
that forces the rest of London into a supporting role.

It's in moments like these that London
has never felt more lonely.

By now, it is dark on every street in England.
And so I slip a bookmark into London,
turn off the city, pour myself a glass of water
and return to the age-old literary device

of Googling myself. Hitting refresh
the same way our parents threw stones into lakes,
the same way cartoonists always start with the eyes

then return every couple of lines
and add another invisible circle.

Devil at the End of Love

Chrissy Williams

Surprised at the birth of stars,
passions built on noble gases,
the Devil objects. An Angel comes
full of light and carbon compounds
to chase him off with promise,
possibility lit in a single word.
Devil says WIE HEIßT DAS WORT?
and the Angel laughs into infinity.
"Do you not know the only Word?
The Word that wings joyfully
through the universe? The Word
that expiates all guilt, the eternal
Word?" Now is the time for violins,
morsing out in bold metallic bursts
as hands are held, silences broken.
Devil says WIE HEIßT DAS WORT
and there is a solid flash of horizon,
as hearts explode in unending
strokes, a complete understanding
of ourselves. Joy. Flashes of light.
  The singular reality tonight:

```
        \ I I I I I I I I /
        – L I E B E –
        / I I I I I I I I \
```

from Speak to Strangers
Gemma Seltzer

Day 6

Your hair falls in the same way mine does, over one shoulder, uneven ends trailing to your chest. You're roughly a head taller than me but that might be your shoes. A name like yours is unnatural shortened but still, you have chosen this label that trips me up. It's too immediately familiar. You speak about a new opportunity, not with wistfulness but restlessness. It will tie you down and you want absolute freedom. In you, there is a bright glowing place. I'd like to see you stand upright, holding a cigarette between angled fingers, hair piled on your head.

Day 34

In South America, women weave fireflies in their hair. In London, two men stare at the tube map above my head, make a decision on their route, then realise they are travelling in the wrong direction. Between them – not literally – they have six teenagers who call them Dad or Dave or Uncle Michael. The girls own hair straighteners and friendship bands. A lone boy doesn't know what to say to them all. There's chanting and falling into seats. I help them follow the navy blue line to Russell Square. It's not far, I tell them. Change here, mind the gap.

Day 71

You appear to me hazy because I am too ingrained in the dense earth of my life to be uprooted. When we speak, you frown and shrug, maybe not in that order, or maybe you didn't do that at all. You are bespectacled and prone to laugh. I, on the other hand, feel morose, with eyes inclined to spill. Last week, I tried to ask questions of someone I knew wouldn't answer and knew I knew that too. At the time, I thought this was meaningful but now I think that there are things I will never know about people.

A Hornchurch Commuter

Luke Wright

It's Winter and I leave my home in darkness
to schlep down Suttons Gardens, Stations Lane,
then past the rows of houses lost to commerce:
the florist, cabbies, bookies, café, train.

They call this game the rat race but it's not —
these sad and silty mornings pocked with sighs;
there's nothing fast about this way of life —
just deep ruts cut slow into the mind's eye.

I spend my Mondays living for the weekend —
who doesn't here, eh, that's the way it works;
that's why we brought our families to the suburbs
to live on London's green and pleasant skirt.

Inside this fizzing fence of motorway,
our tiny crumbs of Essex neatly mortgaged,
a low-rent Metroland for boys done good;
a place to deckchair doze in heavy August.

And for that right we clatter down these traintracks
through greyish sprawl from Dagenham to Bow
where London's mouth lies waiting. Grin and bear it:
inhale, exhale then underground you go.

Boston Tea
Stephanie Leal

December 16, 1773

Sixteen sips from Chinese porcelain
espy the arbitrary day, the decisive act.

History began mohawking the bay:
vulcanizing sand dunes

cracking into champagned water,
bubbling with stamped-out Liberty,

the smuggling thief; a unanimous
continental conspiracy

to remember the misrepresentation,
remember the gunpowder;

convulsing welkin
obscures feathered headdress.

The tea still washes up
on the shores of Boston;

nothing was damaged or stolen
except a padlock

that was accidentally broken,
but anonymously replaced one week after.

Clubbing

Inua Ellams

It begins with shackling necklaces across throats:
the distorted custom of wearing amulets to battle,
talismans to war; we are new hunters, wear jeans

for camouflage, clutch mobile phones like spears,
journey to the village/town/city square, meet
the rest of the tribe, mostly in short skirts, armed

with stilettos, armoured by Chanel. Dusk thickens,
the customary bickering between us commences
through the jungle vines of power lines/stampede

of zebra crossings/night growth of streets bustling,
our ritual is natural, till the traders come. Greater
armed, they divide with such ease that most of us

are taken. Those who resist are swayed by liquor
deals, sailed to darkness where the master spins
a tune not our own. We move stiffly to it as minds

force indifference, but spines have a preference
for drums. Rage building, we make our melody,
fight to find our feet until the master tries to mix

our movement with his song... but the rhythm is
uneven and the tempo, wrong. Against its waves,
we raise voices in anger, fists in protest, dancers

in the tide, militant against the music, a million
men marching through seas. But we still know
how to cross water; the ocean holds our bones,

explains our way of navigating past bouncers
like breeze into night's air, where clouds pass
like dark ships and find us beached, benched

with parched lips, loose-limbed and looking
to light. Now, the best thing about clubbing
is not this, or the struggle to make hips sway

just so, not the need to charge cloakrooms
as if through underground railroads. No.
Best thing about clubbing is the feeling

of freedom on the ride home.

A Glass of Water

Tim Cresswell

They say this glass of London water passed through eight bodies
                                                before mine.
Starting near Heathrow. A Sikh cabby. The morning shift.
Then teacher between classes, a young woman, Kiwi, fit to burst.
A Southall market seller, bagging mangoes and bitter gourd.
A man who lives on a Brentford boat, pissing straight into the
                                                Thames.
Kevin, who drank six pints last night and has a killer thirst.
A gardener at Kew tending orchids, blooming just one day.
Carrie, just up from bed, still red-raw from energetic sex.
And old man Andy, up the road, downing morning pills.
They say my body is sixty percent this. Blood. Spit. Plasma. Piss.
A constant whoosh and sluice. Tidal. Tethered to the moon
like a walking, thinking sea. I half expect to stretch and flop —
a water balloon about to pop and drench my neighbour
on the Tube with my multitude of juices
in waves — six small splashes then a seventh monster —
enough to drown the Underground.

Ghosts

George Ttoouli

All the houses in this city
have ghosts. The shops in Little India
and the stalls in China Town all
full of ghosts. Sometimes you'll see a pickup

full of ghosts, Sri Lankans, Tamils,
making their way to a construction site,
under bridges or in alleys
howling with air conditioning units.

I found a line in one ghost's poem which read,
You can't take the kampongs out
of the people, and to me it sounded
defiant, but later I learned what it meant.

She was cute; her dad worked
for the government. At night I swim
with the ghosts in the pool by the flats,
their wakes skimming behind their empty shapes.

Check-up
Kirsten Irving

My pulse is not so much normal as superb,
and Dr Bryson asks me to extend my legs, then
hold them above the table, clamped together in a barb,

remarking, *yup, you could see those crushing a man.*
It's a joke. I'm not the kind and he's at my throat,
murmuring, *good shape, good definition.*

The olfactory check requires a flashlight
and I tilt my head, letting the bulb probe the glued
flaps of my nose, as the doctor pencils a note.

I tell him bright lights, even now, undo
all of the inhibitors in me. My mind gropes
so quickly for the inquisition chair I was slung into.

You should be pleased, he says. *All of us hope
our memories will last. Your kind can at least
select and cut.* I tell him, *no,* though the rope

and the pincers crouch in my sleep like beasts,
I do not want to lose them, do not want
to forget and return, once again greased

for the mission. I tell him about the marble font

at the cathedral, about the nettles springing
up through the park, gravel, crushed paper, mint,

and say before they placed a hot metal ring
on my eyes, before they sent my remains
back to you as scrap, I never noticed such things.

Bryson motions me to dress. He explains
my new regimen and I agree to everything.
My respray is dry. It looks like rain.

Eating Out

Joe Dunthorne

There are dumpsters simply brimming
with left overs and send backs,
black sacks full of nummy slop:
coconut pannacotta
truffle honey mozzarella
California bouillabaisse
and even if you mush
the food together
it still tastes pretty good
but then, you see,
there are these down-by-luck
table-salt of the earth types:
smelling like asparagus piss,
no money, no grub,
little half-healed cuts on their nose bridges,
and anyhow
you'd think they might be allowed
to lick a strand of marinated pig fat
from the inside of a bin bag
but no, because the nosh,
even when it's been tossed out,
still represents the chef
- it's still product -
and they say a restaurant's reputation
is only equal to its clientele

and, on occasion, these homeless chaps
shout abuse through letter boxes
so the really good restaurants
have a cage,
a big steel cage in the alley out the back,
to protect the scraps
from these poor sods
with their bellies cramping
and their sunburnt eyelids
and so, I mean,
it makes you terribly helpless really,
forty slightly overdone scallops
going to rot in a cage, imagine.

from NOT AN ESSAY
Heather Phillipson

Cities hardwire brains for work.
The mind's floorboards are 1mm thick after the city's repetitive planing. The city is where bodies bump without sticking. The view inside here is endlessly fulfilling. It's all the questions to a lifetime's answers. It's a baking hot evening. The city comes from nowhere, extending in several directions. It's been formulated out of scraps of everything. Hundreds of little figures fleeing before the climax, as Breughel might paint it. The city is shapeless, despite the fact we know what's around all corners. ACTION! It is all, even if we miss it by moments.

experiential cross
Michael Egan

glass against glass   box within box
simple wall cross to keep and hold
defines   just right for hanging
up   off   from
in its own   with its whiteness
in its own   with its wrapping
take from   take with   take this
and drill it in to place
aside   one is wood   one wooden
another steel   stolen   one with D-A-V-I-D
written across   and all things
get remembered   forgotten
end up in another box
beneath   away   hidden in a cave.

A Silence Opens
David Caddy

No one I know or heard of
wants to live there now.
There are no signposts to the road.
The village bank closed long ago.

This is the view you laughed at,
sometimes, at least, weeping with,
trying to dovetail into a gentle
and condensed living.

When you left the season was high
with heartsease, lovage, tansy, self-heal.
Now it spawns gestures of recognition, mild
complaint, the bark of transience.

Gnarled old-timers fretful, densely frugal,
hateful of the French and Labour,
long for pitchfork days, leaning into gates,
following distant hares, coursing.

Effort and loss redundant in a moment's
blink, a ledger cross, some lack
or fickle twist and the holding grows thin
at the end of a dwindling track.

annotated silence

NATHAN PENLINGTON

*

†

‡

§

* a footnote to nothing
† like love unspoken
‡ hinted at by tiny gestures
§ hung in space

Two Moons for Mongs

Ross Sutherland

Frosty mongs bosh shots of Scotch
on London's Brook Common,
rock-off to soppy mono toss;
lost songs of London:
Town of Bop.

No motor. No lolly. No job to mock.
From tons of pot
down to Jon's bong only
(too strong for Tony,
only Tony don't know so).

Gordon's cold brown cosh
of old hotdog
now looks *so good.*
Tony scoffs lot; sods off
to look for polos.

Johnny shows Gordon how to body-pop;:
slow Robocop foxtrot
to Bobby Brown.
Scott robs Holly's shock blowjob story;
lots of ho ho ho follows.

Two o'clock:

Tony growls *bon mot* bollocks
from London's soft throng of woods;
lost moth for God's two moons.
Poor Tony looks down, drops
Pollock on both boots.

On plots so holy,
old dogs poo boldly.
Goons do loops of blocks,
too cold for words.

Gordy pops bon bons.
Jon spots...

Bono.

Both gobs go
'O'.

The Winddown
Roddy Lumsden

This everything
is something about dying. This gallon heart misheard as galleon heart.

This boding. This gadding cause. This vibey scorn. This advice: *learn*

your best songs young. This, the body, its clock sorely needing wound.

CREDITS

'Hwaet' and 'Scop' by Meghan Purvis from *Beowulf* (2013); 'Austerity Rules' and 'Such is the importance of shipwrecks' by Steve Spence from *Limits of Control* (2011); 'When Paperboys Roamed the Earth', 'Things To Do Before You Leave Town' and 'Two Moons for Mongs' by Ross Sutherland from *Things To Do Before You Leave Town* (2009); 'The Machine' and 'The Winddown' by Roddy Lumsden from *The Bells of Hope* (2012); 'Wild Boar of New York' and 'Coney Island Cribs' by Sarah Hesketh from *Napoleon's Travelling Bookshelf* (2009); 'Gaddafi Gaddafi Gaddafi' and 'Arvo Crash' by Hannah Silva from *Forms of Protest* (2013); 'Schwarzheide, 1986' and 'The Method' by Rob Stanton from *The Method* (2011); 'Rare Metallophytes' and 'A Glass of Water' by Tim Cresswell from *Soil* (2013); 'Kapoor's Temenos' by Siddhartha Bose from *Digital Monsoon* (2013); 'Honeymoon After Tikrit', 'Perhaps Other Reasons' and '(Re.vision)' by Emily Critchley from *Love / All That / & OK* (2011); 'Carbon' by Melissa Lee-Houghton from *A Body Made of You* (2011); 'Human Form' and 'Time Permitting' by Oliver Dixon from *Human Form* (2013); 'Signs & Shivers' by Iain Sinclair from *Adventures in Form: A Compendium of Poetic Forms, Rules & Constraints* (2012, ed. Tom Chivers); 'Kid' by Abigail Oborne from *Generation* Txt (2006, ed. Tom Chivers); 'Richard Branson' and 'Poem Looked Up on Google Streetview' by Ross Sutherland from *Emergency Window* (2012); 'Poem in Which You Ask How You Can Tell Real Pearls from High Quality Fakes' and 'Communion' by Claire Trévien from *The Shipwrecked House* (2013); *Count from Zero to One Hundred* by Alan Cunningham (2013); 'Long Letter; Short Farewell' by SJ Fowler & Sam Riviere from *Enemies: The Selected Collaborations of SJ Fowler* (2013); 'Our Glasnost Love' by Chris McCabe from *Speculatrix* (2014); *NOT AN ESSAY* by Heather Phillipson (2012); 'Gists and Piths' and 'Ghosts' by George Ttoouli from *Static Exile* (2009); 'Charismatic Megafauna' by Tamsin Kendrick from *Charismatic Megafauna* (2009); 'A Volta for the Sonnet as a Drag Queen' by Sophie Mayer from *Adventures in Form: A Compendium of Poetic Forms, Rules & Constraints* (2012, ed. Tom Chivers); 'Church Hill' and 'A Silence Opens' by David Caddy from *Man in Black* (2008); 'Spring-Summer Collection' by James Wilkes from *Weather A System* (2009); 'On Raymond's Bike' by Susie Gordon from *Peckham Blue* (2004); 'Beautiful Girls' and 'Heaven' by Melissa Lee-Houghton from *Beautiful Girls* (2013); 'Animal City' by Siddhartha Bose from *Kalagora* (2010); *Holophin* by Luke Kennard (2012); 'Dr Wha' by James Robertson from *Where Rockets Burn Through: Contemporary Science Fiction Poems from the UK* (2012, ed. Russell Jones); 'On Unpredictable Weather Conditions' by Heather Phillipson from *City State: New London Poetry* (2009, ed. Tom Chivers); 'boats' and 'experiential cross' by Michael Egan from *Steak & Stations* (2010); 'Incorrigibly Plural' by Simon Barraclough from *Bonjour Tetris* (2010); 'Devil at the End of Love' by Chrissy Williams from *Where Rockets Burn Through: Contemporary Science Fiction Poems from the UK* (2012, ed. Russell Jones); *Speak to Strangers* by Gemma Seltzer (2011); 'A Hornchurch Commuter' by Luke Wright from

Mondeo Man (2013); 'Boston Tea' by Stephanie Leal from *Metrophobia* (2009); 'Clubbing' by Inua Ellams from *City State: New London Poetry* (2009, ed. Tom Chivers); 'Check-up' by Kirsten Irving from *Where Rockets Burn Through: Contemporary Science Fiction Poems from the UK* (2012, ed. Russell Jones); 'Eating Out' by Joe Dunthorne from *Generation Txt* (2006, ed. Tom Chivers); 'annotated silence' by Nathan Penlington from *Adventures in Form: A Compendium of Poetic Forms, Rules & Constraints* (2012, ed. Tom Chivers).